BOY YOGI

DEVEO STUDIO www.deveostudio.com
Front cover image and coloring by Radu Muresan
Book design by Reka Karpat
First printing 2023.

Dedicated to Shivabalayogi, the Boy Yogi, and in loving memory of my sister, Sarah Jill Gray, whose generosity made this publication possible.

Special thanks to many individuals, including the following, for invaluable encouragement and guidance: Shivabalananda - India, Jay Mazo and Tom Palotas - AZ, Asha - DE, Arthur - NY, elle-Anandi and Surya - VA, Deepa - CA, Ryan - MD, Tesla - SD, Maria - Norway, Aljosa - Croatia, Reka , Ciprian, Horatiu, Radu at Deveo Studio - Romania.

Abridged from The Boy Yogi, 2005, Sriharikota, India and adapted from Chapters 1-4 of Shri Shri Shri Shivabalayogi Maharaj, Life & Spiritual Ministration, by Brigadier Hanut Singh MVC,1981, Bangalore, India. The Boy Yogi book, read by a teenager, has been on Youtube.com since 2018.

Abridged and written by:
Jane Gail Germaine Gray,
Offering meditation to adults and children for nearly 40 years.
Yogaville, Buckingham, VA
meditate-shivabalayogi.org

This is the true story, about the teenager Sathyaraju, who sat in meditation for twelve years; twenty-three hours daily for eight years, and twelve hours daily for four years, to become the greatest yogi, Shri Shri Shri Shivabalayogi Maharaj (1935-1994).

Sathyaraju lives in a poor Indian family of weavers with his mother, Parvathamma, his grandfather, Goli, two older sisters and an older brother.

Their home is in the little village of Adivarapupeta, surrounded by groves of coconut and palmyra trees near a small canal, Godavari. Sathyaraju's father died when he was just two years old. Goli finds it difficult to support his recently widowed daughter, and her four children.

At six years old, Sathyaraju must work at home before attending school. He wakes at 5 a.m., bathes and eats a rice and curd (yogurt) breakfast. Then he works hard at the loom, weaving brightly colored cloth, the specialty of his family.

After lunch, he goes to school from 10 a.m. to about 4 p.m. When school is over, he goes out to play until dinner at 6 p.m.

After dinner, Sathyaraju talks with his grandfather for about an hour. He tells him everything that happened that day. Goli listens to him with interest, always giving him valuable guidance. At 7 p.m., he goes out to play swords with his friends, or he joins a group singing praises to God. He goes to bed by 10 p.m. It is a hard life for such a young child, but not different from the lives of poor children in most villages.

Sathyaraju adores his grandfather and Goli deeply loves his grandson. He trusts his Grandfather, always following his advice. One day, eight year old Sathyaraju is sent to work in a neighboring town. Goli tells him, "You have many relatives there. They may not be considerate. You should behave yourself, and not visit their homes unless invited."

It is 11 o'clock at night, when he finally finishes working. No relatives have invited him for a meal, or to stay the night. He remembers his grandfather's advice. He spends the night sleeping on a shop porch. Early the next morning, he returns home and tells Goli, who is proud of his decision.

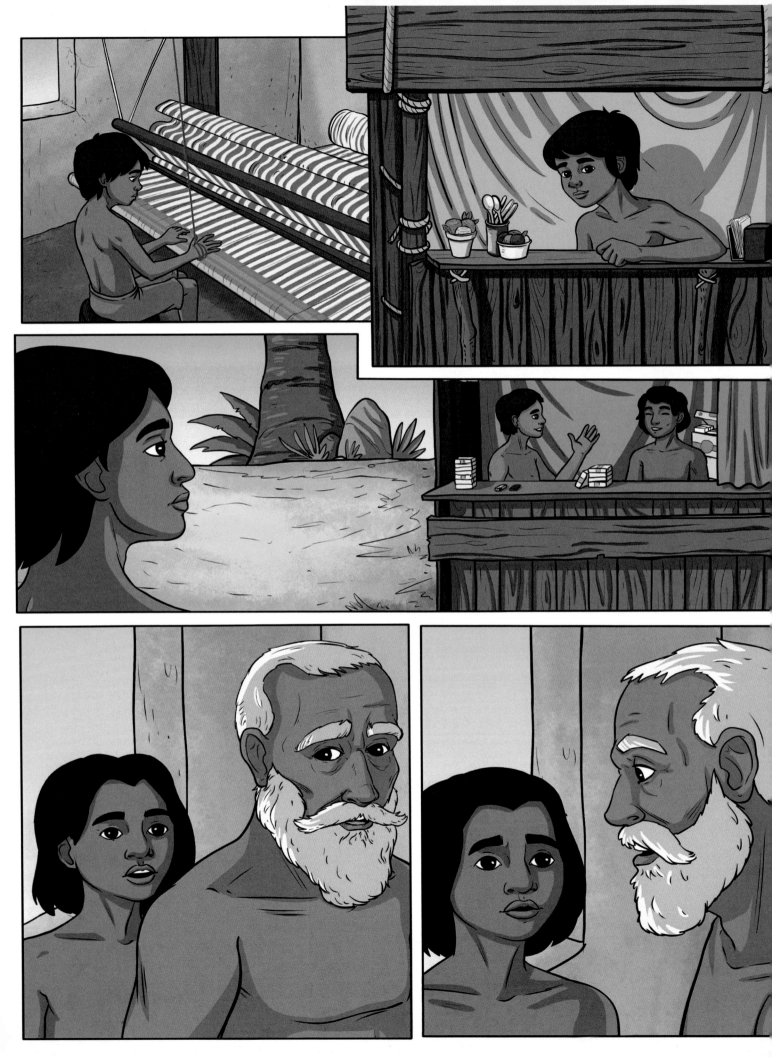

Sathyaraju is a good student, who likes his subjects, and is respected by his friends. At just eight years old, he decides to stop going to school. He wants to spend all his time earning money for his impoverished family. He puts in long, extra hours weaving at the loom, giving all his earnings to his mother and grandfather. In the summer, he earns some extra money selling sherbet and cool drinks.

By the age of 12, he thinks deeply about how to lift his family out of poverty. He sees that some village boys have opened a beedi stand (a cheap cigarette stand), and they are doing well. He discusses the idea with his grandfather. "I would like to open a beedi stand." Goli isn't pleased. He tells him, "Become a cloth salesman. It's a more suitable profession for a member of the community."

Sathyaraju respects his grandfather's opinion. This delays his plans, but he does not give up the idea. One day, he sees a shiny copper coin by the path. This is a sign of good fortune if found this way. He picks it up and touches it first to his right, and then to his left eye. Then he joins a game of marbles with friends. He wins enough marbles to sell for money to open his beedi stand.

Sathyaraju goes to a Holy Shrine and sincerely prays to God for success. He opens the stand. Soon he is making more money than he ever did weaving. The rival stand suddenly closes. All the customers come to his stand. He starts making good profits, giving his earnings to his mother and grandfather. This pleases them. Happy with his success, Sathyaraju plans to expand the business.

7TH AUGUST 1949

On Sunday afternoon August 7, 1949, 14 1/2 year old Sathyaraju is walking to the canal with 11 friends for a bath. Passing by a grove of palmyra trees, three palmyra fruits fall to the ground near them. The boys bring the fruit to Sathyaraju, their leader, who divides the fruit into 12 pieces. He shares equally with his 11 friends, keeping one piece of fruit for himself.

Sathyaraju peels his fruit and is about to eat it. His body starts trembling uncontrollably. A light emerges from the fruit sounding 'Om', the original vibration of the Universe. The Divine Light and sound cover him with waves of great happiness. His body stops trembling and his mind is peaceful.

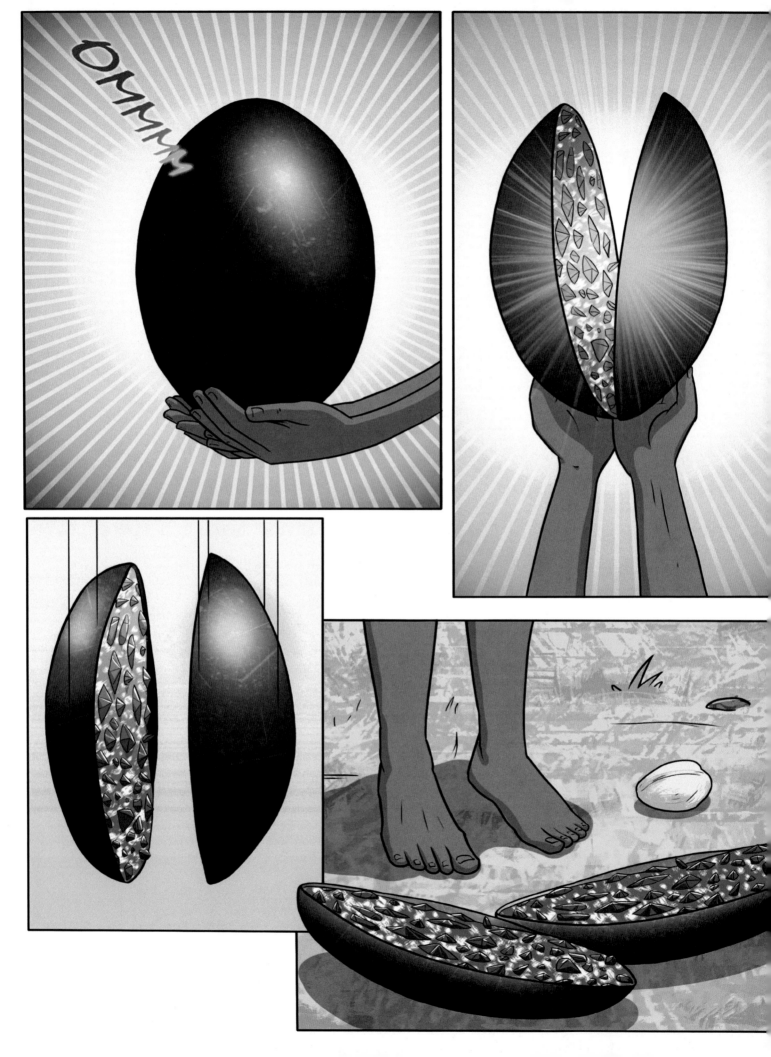

The fruit in his hand vanishes from his view. In its place appears a black Shiva Lingam stone, symbol of Lord Shiva. It emits dazzling light, and the sound of 'Om'. It breaks into two pieces and falls to the ground along with the fruit.

Standing before him is a well-built, dark-skinned Yogi over 7 feet tall. He has an attractive face with large beautiful eyes. His long, matted hair is piled on top of his head like the ancient Yogis. He wears a necklace of Rudraksha beads, 108 prayer beads, with a small Shiva Linga resting on his broad chest. He wears a dhoti, a trouser-like cloth worn by men. A brilliance radiates from him, blotting out Sathyaraju's vision. He sees only the Yogi, nothing else.

The Divine Guide says, "Sit down." Sathyaraju responds, "Why do you want me to sit down?" Divine Guide says, "You will be told. Sit down." Sathyaraju sits down. Divine Guide says, "Sit in lotus posture." Sathyaraju responds. "I don't know how to sit in lotus posture." Divine Guide places each foot on the opposite thigh. Divine Guide says, "Close your eyes." Sathyaraju says, "Why do you want me to close my eyes?" Divine Guide responds, "Close your eyes and I'll tell you."

He closes his eyes. Divine Guide touches him at the brow center and gently taps his head. Sathayaraju loses human consciousness. He enters God-consciousness, absorbed only by the Shiva Linga's dazzling light.

He is 14 1/2 years old, beginning the 12 years of Tapas Meditation, on August 7, 1949, facing East for the first 4 years.

His friends think Sathyaraju is acting. They first tease, then pull and slap him. With no reaction, they smear him with palmyra juice and mud. They carry him to the canal and dunk him. Still no response. Worried they'll be blamed for his condition, they clean him up and carry him back to the canal bank. Then they run home to tell his relatives.

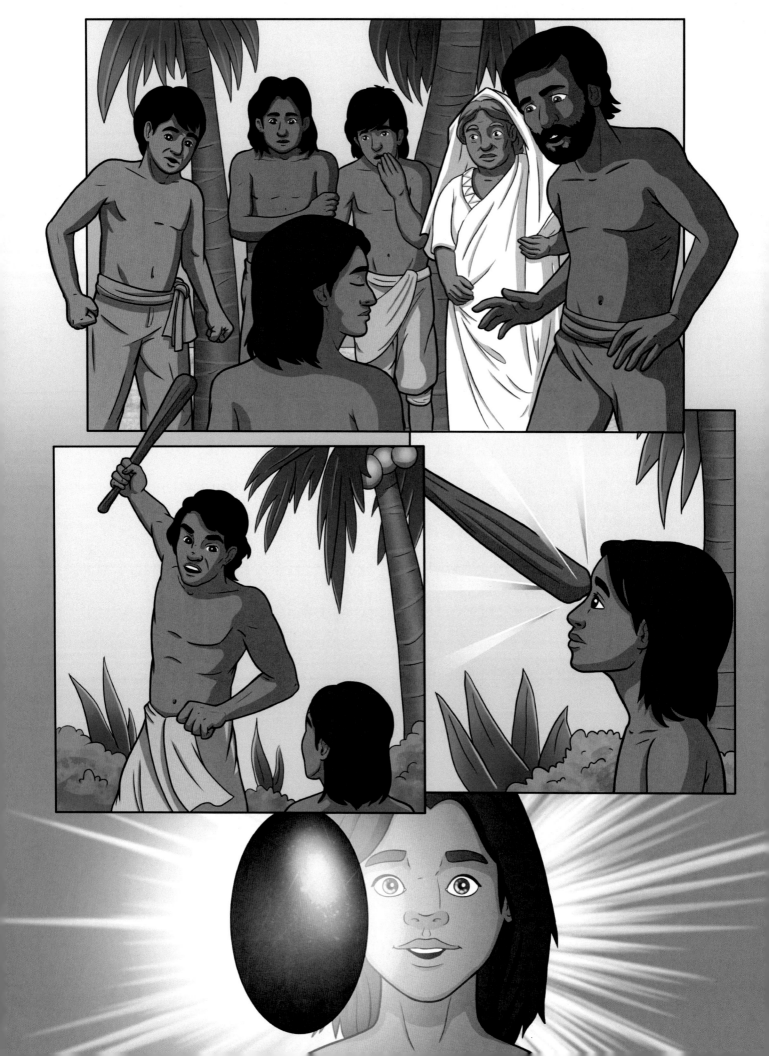

His mother and grandfather are still away in town. So, his uncle, with a few friends, goes to the spot where Sathyaraju is meditating. They stand around watching his unusual behavior. One man suggests that Sathyaraju is probably possessed by a ghost or spirit. In order to drive out the entity, he starts hitting him repeatedly with a stout wooden club. When the club accidently hits between Sathyaraju's eyebrows, his deep meditation and Shiva Linga vision stop. Between the eyebrows is the exact spot where Divine Guide touched him.

Sathyaraju gains enough consciousness to recognize his uncle. He asks his uncle for a dhoti to wear in place of his shorts. His uncle gives him the cloth that he is carrying, and Sathyaraju ties it in a dhoti. Two men, one on each side, barely manage to carry him home. At home, he finds his legs are too stiff to step up onto the verandah. So, the two men take hold of him and try to take him inside. But his stiffened legs won't go through the doorway. After trying for an hour, they finally give up, and seat him on the verandah.

News about Sathyaraju spreads through the village. Soon a crowd gathers, and bothers him with questions. He doesn't respond. They end up talking amongst themselves, about whether or not he's possessed by a ghost, or is a holy man. Only one person suggests that Sathyaraju had been transformed into a Yogi.

People start leaving at 8 p.m. By 11 o'clock, those remaining are mostly asleep. The divine vision of the Shiva Linga continues in front of his eyes, along with the 'Om' sound. Sathyaraju decides to return to the canal bank where the Divine experiences first happened. One boy tries to follow him, but he hides from him.

He goes back to the same spot where his Divine Guide first made him sit, but is unable to close his eyes. This doesn't stop him from meditating. He is fully absorbed in the divine vision of the Shiva Linga, even with open eyes. Soon after he arrives at the canal bank, a heavy rain begins, and continues through the night. Though completely soaked, he doesn't consider moving to a protected place. The next morning, some villagers see that he is drenched. Two men carry him to sit under a banyan tree near the village. They place a palmyra leaf umbrella over him to keep off the rain..

Sathyaraju's eyes are still open. He is aware of activity around him, yet pays no attention to it. The bright vision of the Shiva Linga remains steady, unchanging before his eyes. He sees familiar faces and barely remembers who they are, whether family, friends or villagers. The touch of Divine Guide has blotted out all earthly ties. Though it rains all day, he continues to meditate under the palmyra umbrella, totally absorbed in the vision. Later, villagers build a pandal, a shelter of palmyra leaves, and he moves there.

Parvathamma and Goli have been away for two days. Alarmed to hear about Sathyaraju, they rush to the canal bank. They call out, "Sathyaraju, Sathyaraju, Sathyaraju," and soon find him at his pandal. His mother, nearly hysterical, weeps loudly, hugging him to her chest. She cries out, "What has happened to you?" Sathyaraju gains consciousness because of her loud crying and sobbing. With tears flowing from her eyes, she begs him, "Please return home with me." Sathyaraju's mind is totally detached from worldly relationships, and unmoved by her tears and pleading. He calmly tells her, "I have started on the search for Divine, and will not leave this holy path to go back home."

Finding that Sathyaraju is resolved to continue on his chosen path, his grandfather blesses him. Goli tells him, "You have chosen an excellent path and should be determined to stick to it."

After this brief conversation, Sathyaraju closes his eyes and passes into God-consciousness. The grief stricken mother can't bear to leave him and return home alone. She remains nearby, and every so often, she will look at him. One time, when she looks toward him, an enchanting vision of God's Trinity (Trimurti) flashes before her eyes. Thinking it is her imagination, she rubs her eyes. The vision is still there in all its dazzling beauty. Now, everywhere she looks she only sees God's Trinity. This vision makes her feel that Sathyaraju is under Divine protection. She needn't worry about him any longer. This brings her peace, and she returns home happy and content.

Most believe that Sathyaraju is a Bala (Boy) yogi, like this village woman. Early in the morning, she faithfully offers flowers, incense, and a coconut, while he meditates. She distributes the broken coconut pieces as prasad (blessed food). But others wait to torment Balayogi when no one is around, like some boys who come to beat him up.

Late one night, a cruel individual sets Balayogi afire, while he is meditating. Balayogi feels nothing at the time, but the flames cause deep and painful burns on his hands and legs. Though in excruciating pain, he continues meditating. When a kind old man from the village hears about this, he prepares an ointment. He comes daily and applies the ointment, while Balayogi meditates, and quietly leaves. Due to his treatment, the wounds heal, but scars are left on his hands and legs.

One evening, two men decide to test the intensity of Balayogi's deep meditation. One of them pulls Balayogi's legs out of meditation posture. Then he attempts to wake him, by opening one eyelid. Balayogi continues to meditate undisturbed. When he sees that Balayogi's deep meditation is genuine, he feels awful for what he has done. He tries through the night to close the eyelid, and put the legs back, but fails. When Balayogi awakes from meditation in the morning, the man begs for forgiveness. Balayogi smiles and readily forgives him.

Balayogi puts up with these torments for 2 months, and finally gets fed up. He has heard of an Ashram in the neighboring village, where a holy man resides. He leaves at 10:30 one night, and walks to the Ashram. He tries to resume his Tapas Meditation, but the Ashram requirements and officials prevent him from doing so. He doesn't feel accepted there, so only stays one day, and returns home by 10:30 that night.

He doesn't go back to his usual meditation spot. He goes to meditate under a banyan tree on his uncle's property. The next morning, the villagers find that Balayogi is back. They are overjoyed, and come for his blessings.

In November of 1949, a terrific cyclone, with pouring rain and harsh winds, swept across the countryside for 3 hours. Trees are uprooted and houses collapse. The whole area is flooded, with people in great distress. Parvathamma fears for the safety of her son. The worried mother rushes out into the raging storm. A large branch torn off by the wind hits her head. Though stunned by the blow, she reaches the banyan tree where her son is sitting. To her astonishment, she finds the spot under the tree is totally calm and peaceful. Balayogi is in deep meditation, undisturbed by the storm.

Relieved, she goes and sits nearby him. The storm eventually subsides. In the dawn light, she sees the swarms of large red ants. The ants have taken shelter in the area where Balayogi is meditating, clinging to his body. Upset, she immediately starts brushing them off. But he signals her to stop and leave them alone.

While Balayogi is meditating under the banyan tree, many are coming for his blessings. But he is still bothered by those waiting for his caretakers to leave at dusk. One day, he is thinking about how to solve this problem. He decides to move to the village burial ground. Such people will be afraid to follow him there, especially at night, and he might have some peace.

He is correct that these people avoid the burial grounds, particularly at night. He is left alone, only for a short time. The place is swarming with insects and rodents that live off the flesh of the buried, dead bodies. Balayogi is in deep meditation and not moving. He appears to be dead, so they bite him causing many wounds. During his daily midnight bath in the canal, the fish nibble on the open wounds. It has been 15 days since he moved to burial grounds. While walking for his midnight bath, a deadly black cobra rears up and bites him. Blood starts dripping from the wound.

Balayogi ignores the cobra bite, and returns to meditating in the burial grounds. At first, the snake's venom causes blotches of discolored skin. Then infection sets in, with decaying skin giving off a foul smell. He is suffering extreme pain and discomfort.

Discouraged and frustrated by all that he has gone through, Balayogi decides that yogic life isn't for him. It is better to return home and lead a normal life. Afterall, he hasn't chosen this yogic path, but was told to do so by his Divine Guide. With these thoughts in his mind, he gets up from meditation one evening, and starts for home.

His Divine Guide appears, standing under a tree, blocking his way. Divine Guide smiles slightly and says, "Where are you going?" Balayogi says, "I am going home." Divine Guide asks, "Why?" He tells him all his troubles since he started his yogic practice, including the present suffering from the snake bite. He continues, "I can't meditate any longer. I'm thinking of stopping and going home." Divine Guide listens in silence, while looking at him. Divine Guide says, "I want you to go back and not give up your Tapas Meditation for any reason." Divine Guide gives Balayogi a healing prayer for the wounds and then disappears.

He obeys his Divine Guide and decides to never give up his Tapas Meditation. He repeats the healing prayer and his normal health returns.

Balayogi is doing his Tapas Meditation sitting on the bare ground. It is customary to do Tapas Meditation sitting on a deer or tiger skin seat. One visitor, who comes for his blessing, inquires if he needs anything. Balayogi asks him to send a tiger skin. When a man delivers the tiger skin, he finds the ground damp where Balayogi sits. In order to keep the tiger skin dry, he has a wooden platform built with a pandal hut on it. This elevated seat relieves Balayogi from the afflictions of the ants, insects and rodents, and he can meditate more peacefully.

Another man is deeply impressed by the young Balayogi. He wants to build him a more permanent, comfortable structure on private land. Around October, 1950, the Dhyana Mandir (meditation temple) is complete. About the same time, a man has a well dug near Dhyana Mandir. This well provides pure drinking water for the Balayogi, and also for the villagers.

Balayogi is lifted up in meditation posture, and carried to his new, one room home. There he continues his Tapas Meditation sitting on the tiger skin meditation seat.

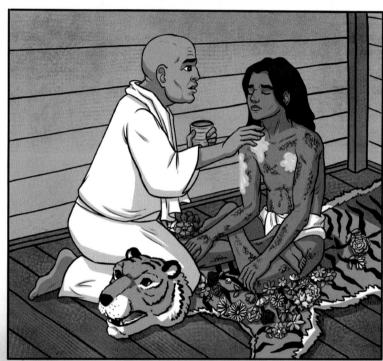

In late 1951, Balayogi's body suffered from a burning foul smell. As he clenches his teeth in intense pain, tears roll down his cheeks. While weeping and twisting in pain, he passes into God-consciousness. Though he can no longer feel the pain, his body is burning and hot to the touch. A great soul, Tapaswiji Maharaj, envisions his suffering, takes a train near his Ashram, and immediately goes to Dhyana Mandir. He applies his special medicated oil all over Balayogi's body. This immediately relieves the burning sensation, and the bad odor disappears.

For 3 years, he endures losing control of his limbs. He isn't able to eat, go for a bath, or care for his body properly. Then in June, 1953, he stops meditating, and just sits around dejected. Divine Guide appears, and asks him what is troubling him. Balayogi tells him all the difficulties that he is having because of his crippled limbs. Divine Guide runs his hands over Balayogi's arms and legs. His crippled limbs are now healed and under his control. Except for the hands, where the fingers are permanently bent. Divine Guide vanishes.

In early October, 1953, Balayogi enters into God-consciousness for a month. During this time, he eats no food and doesn't bathe. Later that month, he was awakened by a tap on his leg. Dazzling light fills the room, and he can barely look at it. A beautiful snow-white figure stands before him. He believes it is Shiva and asks, "Who are you?" Shiva responds, "They call me Shiva, Lord of Peace. I appreciate your determination in your meditation practice. Do you need anything or wish to ask for a blessing?" Balayogi responds, "I don't want anything and wish no blessing." Shiva sits and chats with him for some time. Shiva says, "Your Divine Guide will appear to inform you what to do next." Shiva disappears.

Balayogi, at nearly 19 years old, completed the first Tapas Meditation stage, facing East for 4 years on October 28, 1953.

At midnight, October 29, Divine Guide appears. He says, "You completed facing the East, now you must face North. I will give you a new prayer for facing the North. From this day on, you are to practice mouna (silence)." Divine Guide vanishes.

Balayogi communicates silently with Divine Guide, mostly through thoughts and looks. With others, as well as Divine Guide, he uses gestures moving his body, hands, fingers, face and eyes in different directions.

During October 1954, Divine Guide appears. Balayogi thinks, I want you to take me to the Sun's sphere, so I can see what it's like. Divine Guide nods in agreement, indicating to him not to his open eyes until told to do so. Balayogi follows his directions.

When Balayogi opens his eyes, he is looking down at a landscape that appears to be Earth. He sees mountains with green forests, valleys and rivers. Some mountains are covered with snow.

After a short visit, he wants to return to Earth. He sits on the Divine Guide's palm with closed eyes. They shoot back, almost at the speed of thought. On the way back, they have to pass, very briefly, through the blazing orb of the Sun. Though protected by Divine Guide, he suffered tremendously from the heat. Divine Guide gives him some relief with a dip in every river that they cross. Balayogi only recognizes the Godavari canal near his home.

The Tapas facing North proceeds quickly. At one point, Balayogi enters God-consciousness meditation for 15 days. During this entire period, he enjoys good health, and great bliss in deep meditation.

On the night of August 1, 1955, Shiva appears in a dazzling light. He talks with Balayogi for some time. Shiva asks, "Do you want anything?" Balayogi responds, "I don't want anything." Shiva disappears.

Balayogi completed the 2nd stage of Tapas Meditation facing the North in just 2 years, on August 1, 1955.

Balayogi has a rest for 6 days. At midnight on August 7, Divine Guide appears. He says, "Now you have to sit facing the West. I am letting you know that you will have to face many difficulties and obstacles, seemingly severe. You are not to lose heart and give up. I assure you that when you need help, I will come to your assistance." He gives him the prayer for the Western Direction and disappears.

Immediately, Balayogi develops a severe stomach ache, followed by a burning sensation in the body. Though in extreme pain, he continues meditating. Then, 8 days after starting Tapas of Western Direction, a cow that provides his milk suddenly dies. Subsequently, each cow that is bought or used for his milk dies. Then he is nauseous, throwing up any milk that he tries to consume. Eventually, he is taking no nutrition at all. This can't continue for long with his rigorous Tapas. Fortunately, a woman thinks of substituting Horlicks, a malt drink, for the milk. Balayogi is able to drink this daily until the end of his Tapas of Western Direction.

One midnight, Balayogi opens the door to go for his bath. Lying across the doorway is a huge Naag cobra of shimmering amber color. When the Naag sees him, it rises up, spreads its hood, sways, and hisses at him. He can't find a way to get around it, so he has to step on it. The Naag bites him on the left thigh. Returning from his bath, the same Naag is lying across the doorway. It bites him on the big toe of his right foot, as he steps over it to reenter Dhyana Mandir.

Balayogi closes the door behind him. The poison from the 2 bites affects him immediately. Before he can resume meditation, he falls unconscious onto the wooden platform. The glasses of malt drink slipped inside the window for four days are left untouched. On the 4th day, Divine Guide appears and arouses him from his unconscious state. Weakened from his recent ordeal, he sits up and starts meditating again. Divine Guide disappears.

Mother Parvathamma and other caretakers arrive for their daily visit at 7 p.m. They ask why he didn't drink the malt drinks. He shows them the wounds from the snake bites. He decides to meditate in God-consciousness all the time. Then he won't be upset by news about relatives and friends, or feel bodily pain. He indicates to Parvathamma and the others to leave him entirely alone. They leave and he returns to his Tapas Meditation.

One midnight, while he is bathing, a very old man asks him for a drink of water. Balayogi stops bathing, and pours him a drink from his water pot. After he finishes drinking, he asks Balayogi his name. Balayogi motions with his hand that he doesn't know. The old man then asks Balayogi to lead him home. Balayogi conveys signs that this isn't possible. Suddenly, the old man flares up. "Why do you keep making signs? Why don't you speak to me? Come, you must go with me to the village." The old man grabs him by the arm, and with amazing strength starts dragging him. He is very strong, and Balayogi is weak from Tapas and bodily ailments. In desperation, Balayogi seizes his forked resting stick. With all the strength that he can muster, he strikes the old man's arm to release his grip.

The stick breaks into 2 equal pieces, and Balayogi loses consciousness momentarily. When he recovers, he finds that the old man has disappeared.

He completes his bath and returns to Dhyana Mandir. To his surprise, he finds the broken pieces of the forked resting stick lying on his tiger skin meditation seat. He then realizes that the old man had come to test his commitment to his Tapas practices.

Some days later, about midnight, Balayogi is at the well. A very beautiful girl appears, and asks him for a drink. He draws water from the well with his water pot, and pours it out for her to drink. All the while, she tries various ways to have a conversation with him, but he doesn't respond. Then, she attempts clever methods to make him break his silence and speak to her, but is unsuccessful. Appearing disappointed, she leaves.

Balayogi finishes his bath and walks back to Dhyana Mandir. She is waiting for him, blocking his entrance. He tries to get around her, but she playfully bars his way. He enters another way.

Nearing his doorway, he hears the pleasant tinkling of bells worn by a dancer. Somewhat puzzled, he opens the door. He is very surprised, by finding the same beautiful girl standing in a dance posture. A strange light seems to emanate from her filling the room. Bathed in that glowing light, and standing in a graceful pose, the girl looks divinely beautiful. Suddenly, she breaks into an unearthly, alluring dance.

By now, Balayoigi realizes that he is undergoing another test. He pays no attention to the girl and her dance, and quickly returns to his meditation seat. He closes his eyes, withdraws his mind, and soon is absorbed in God-consciousness.

The next night, May 25, 1956, Divine Guide appears. Balayogi tells him about the visits of the old man and dancing girl. Divine Guide smiles on hearing this. He tells him, "Immerse your mind in God-consciousness, only stop in about a month, when Shiva awakens you."

The next day when Parvathamma visits, he asks her to bring the others. He uses gestures to indicate to them that he will be in God-consciousness for a month, and is not to be disturbed. One finger indicates one month. Next he closes his eyes while sitting in a meditation posture. Then with serious open eyes, he points to himself. Finally, Balayogi waves them away, and locks himself inside Dhyana Mandir.

Balayogi has completed over nine months of Tapas Meditation facing West. His body has been tortured by illness and ailments of all kinds. His skin has cracked open exposing deep wounds that bleed regularly. Balayogi's mind isn't disturbed by such sufferings. Long ago, through his own experiences, he learned that he isn't the body. He is the soul within which isn't affected by such afflictions. Firm in this belief, he continues his Tapas.

Around midnight, on June 25, 1956, he feels a slight tap on his leg, which brings him back to consciousness. As he becomes aware of his surroundings, he sees a dazzling light. Then he feels another tap, and is wide awake. Standing before him are Shankara and Gauri, looking like jungle folk. Balayogi is speechless, filled with joy and wonder, and just keeps gazing at them.

Shankara, with an approving smile, says, "I have been trying to wake you up, but you wouldn't wake up." Balayogi responds, somewhat surprised, "Oh, I didn't know or feel anything till now, when you tapped me." Shankara and Gauri sit opposite him, and talk with him for a while. Shankara says, "You should continue your Tapas until you complete the full 12 years. I will tell you what I want you to do after that time." They both disappear.

The 21 year old Balayogi completed the 3rd stage, perfection of the Western Direction, in less than a year, on June 25, 1956.

The next night, June 26, 1956, Divine Guide appears. Divine Guide says, "You are to sit facing South. Here is the prayer for the Southern direction." He vanishes. The Tapas of the Southern direction continued for a little over 10 months.

In May 1957, Shankara Bhagavan appears before Balayogi. Shankara's appearance indicates that 22 year old Balayogi completed the 4th stage of Tapas Meditation, facing South.

In celebration of his completion of Tapas of all 4 directions, 108 coconuts are broken in each direction. It starts at 7 a.m., and is completed by midnight. When it is over, Balayogi ends his 4 years of mouna by melodiously chanting 'Om'.

The following midnight, Divine Guide appears. Balayogi has believed that Divine Guide was a holy man throughout his eight years of meditation. Now that he has completed all four directions, a doubt arises about Divine Guide's true identity. Balayogi says "Who are you? What is your true identity?" Divine Guide responds, "Don't you know who I am?" He says, "No, I don't know. I am even more perplexed by your behavior and appearance. Suddenly you appear as if out of thin air and then vanish, just as quickly. Your features are the same as Shiva. But Shiva has a white complexion with dazzling light. You are dark-skinned with no dazzling light. This is all puzzling, so I wonder about your actual identity."

Divine Guide says, with an amused smile, "After all I've done for you, you still have a doubt. I'll tell you after you complete the full 12 years of Tapas Meditation. You are to meditate facing East again. Start teaching meditation to seekers, and only remain in God-consciousness for 12 hours, not 24 hours."

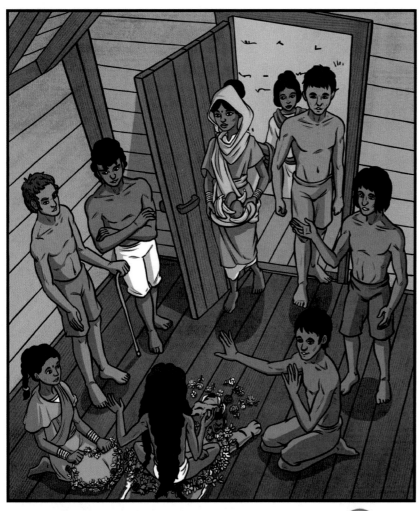

Now that Balayogi is giving public blessings, an increasing number of people crowd into Dhyana Mandir. For the next 3 1/2 years, he meditates from 4 a.m. to 4 p.m., and teaches meditation from 4 p.m. to midnight. At midnight he bathes, and takes a rest from 1 a.m. to 3 a.m.

About January, 1961, he starts losing his appetite for fruit. Eventually, He stops all fruit, and only drinks milk occasionally. On most days, he merely drinks water when he goes to the well for midnight bath. Simultaneously, meditation in God-consciousness starts to increase. Around the beginning of June, 1961, Balayogi becomes totally absorbed in God-consciousness, which lasts through July.

At midnight on August 1st, Divine Guide appears, and arouses Balayogi from his God-consciousness. Divine Guide smiles and says, "You have a doubt about my true identity. All right, now watch closely."

Dazzling light flashes from Divine Guide's body. The dark-skinned Divine Guide disappears. In his place stands white Shankara Bhagavan, Balayogi's chosen form of God. Balayogi then realized that Shankara himself guided him in the form of Divine Guide. Shankara and Mother Parvati, who accompanied him, talk affectionately with Balayogi.

Shankara says, "Your 12 year Tapas Meditation period is over. You are free to go wherever you like and do whatever you wish." Balayogi responds, "I don't wish to go anywhere or do anything in particular." Shankara continues, "You may ask for anything and it shall be granted to you." Balayogi replies, "I desire nothing and will do whatever you want me to do."

Shankara is pleased with Balayogi's answer, and compliments him on his commitment to his Tapas Meditation practice. Shankara says, "From now on your special duty is to travel around, and help others on the spiritual path. Give them blessings. Teach them meditation. Comfort those who are sad or ill. Give them holy ash to heal their body and mind. I will ask you to sit in long meditations, as needed in the future."

Shankara and Parvati affectionately say, "We give you our blessings. Good-bye." They merge into the body of Balayogi. The Balayogi's name changes to Shivabalayogi Maharaj (Shivabalayogi).

OMMMM OMMMM OMMM

As the day for the completion of Balayogi's Tapas draws near, thousands begin streaming into Adivarapupeta for his blessings. By the morning of August 7, 1961, a vast crowd of over 300,000 is assembled around Dhyana Mandir, joyously awaiting the appearance of the Balayogi.

At 8 a.m. Shivabalayogi marks the occasion of his completion of Tapas by melodiously chanting, 'Om' from inside his room. The Dhyana Mandir door swings open, and Shivabalayogi steps outside.

As he comes into view, a mighty roar bursts forth from the elated crowd. Shivabalayogi's legs are wobbly, not used to walking, and his body is weak from the lack of food. Someone helps him to go down the stairs.

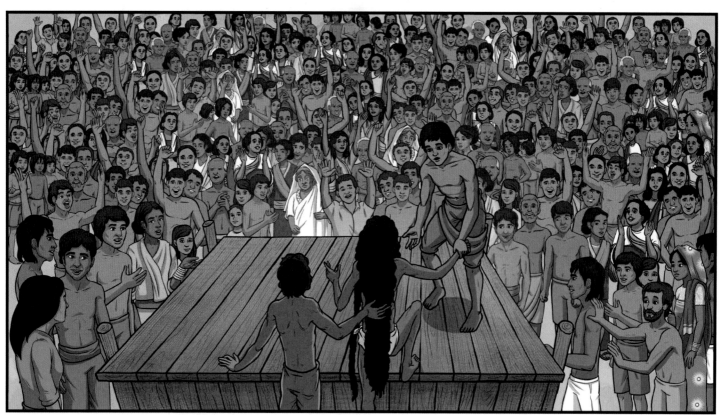

Thunderous cheering and loud hurrahs break out across the countryside from the vast multitude. He is assisted up onto the platform, built for this special occasion.

Standing there with closed eyes, Shivabalayogi silently showers blessings on the thousands who have come for his blessing. They see a Yogi whose emaciated body is almost deformed by the rigors of his Tapas. Yet his body shines with an extraordinary brightness, radiating peace and spiritual grace.

Shivabalayogi gave this message to the crowd of 300,000.
"People should meditate.
They must know themselves.
This will bring peace
to the world."

13804820R00069